Health Solutions
Anxiety

Edited by
Dr Savitri Ramaiah

STERLING PAPERBACKS
An imprint of
Sterling Publishers (P) Ltd.
A-59, Okhla Industrial Area, Phase-II,
New Delhi-110020.
Tel: 26387070, 26386209; Fax: 91-11-26383788
E-mail: sterlingpublishers@airtelmail.in
ghai@nde.vsnl.net.in
www.sterlingpublishers.com

Anxiety
© 2008, Sterling Publishers (P) Ltd.
ISBN 978-81-207-3326-8
Reprint 2008, 2012

All rights are reserved.
No part of this publication may be reproduced, stored in a retrieval system or transmitted, in any form or by any means, mechanical, photocopying, recording or otherwise, without prior written permission of the original publisher.

Printed and Published by Sterling Publishers Pvt. Ltd.,
New Delhi-110 020.

Information for this series, has been provided by *Health Update*, a monthly bulletin of the Society for Health Education and Learning Packages. The Update is intended to provide you with knowledge to adopt preventive measures and cooperate with the doctor during illness for better outcome of treatment.

Contributors

Allopathy
Dr Savitri Ramaiah
(Member-Secretary, Society for Health Education and Learning Packages, New Delhi)

Ayurveda
Dr V N Pandey
(Former Director, Central Council for Research in Ayurveda and Siddha, New Delhi)

Homoeopathy
Dr Sangeeta Chopra
(Consultant Homoeopathy, New Delhi)

Nature Cure
Dr Sambhashiva Rao
(Former Chief Medical Officer, Institute of Naturopathy, Bangalore)

Unani
Hakim Mohammed Khalid Siddiqui
(Director, Central Council for Research in Unani, New Delhi)

Preface

Health Solutions is an easy-to-read reference series put together by *Health Update* and assisted by a team of medical experts who offer the latest perspectives on body health.

Each book in the series enhances your knowledge on a particular health issue. It makes you an active participant by giving multiple perspectives to choose from — allopathy, ayurveda, homoeopathy, nature cure and unani.

This book is intended as a home adviser but does not substitute a doctor.

The opinions are those of the contributors, and the publisher holds no responsibility.

Contents

Preface	7
Introduction	11
Allopathy	13
Ayurveda	45
Homoeopathy	53
Nature Cure	65
Unani	77
Definitions	85
References	86

Introduction

Anxiety is a problem that affects almost everyone at some point of time or the other. It is a normal reaction to a stressful situation and is, therefore, short-lived. It is important to remember that anxiety can exist alone or in combination with other symptoms of several emotional disorders.

Surroundings, suppressed emotions and physical causes can cause anxiety. These conditions can be broadly divided into three categories — anxiety states, phobic disorders and post-traumatic stress disorders.

Increased irritability, headache, tremors and hyper activity of the autonomic system point to an anxious state of mind.

Allopathy

Anxiety is not a disease but a symptom. Most people have anxiety at some time or the other in their life. Usually, it is a normal reaction to a stressful situation and is therefore short-lived. Anxiety can adversely affect your work if it occurs often. It is important to remember that anxiety can exist alone or in combination with other symptoms of several emotional disorders. It is the most common feature of majority of psychiatric illnesses.

How common is anxiety?

Anxiety is one of the most under-reported conditions largely due to ignorance. It is difficult to estimate the number of people suffering from anxiety because most people suffering from anxiety do not consult a doctor. This is mainly because many people believe that only "mentally sick" people need to consult with a psychiatrist. In the United States, an estimated five per cent of the total population suffer from anxiety. Anxiety is more common among women than men. Some studies have indicated that anxiety may also run in families.

Why should I go to a psychiatrist? I am not mentally sick.

It is believed that the number of people suffering from anxiety is increasing at an alarming rate due to pressures of modern life. However, some specialists feel that there is no conclusive evidence to prove that anxiety is on the increase. According to them, increased awareness and the desire to live life fully have resulted in more number of people seeking help for anxiety.

Box 1. Anxiety and fear
<ul><li>Anxiety is the result of psychological and physiological processes in the body.</li><li>Anxiety is not the same as fear although it is related to it.</li><li>Anxiety is the response to danger that warns you from "within" — as an instinct — that there is danger and you may lose control of the situation.</li><li>Fear is the reaction to real danger that can cause harm.</li><li>Fear is usually short-lived. Anxiety lasts longer.</li><li>It is normally difficult to assess whether your reaction is due to anxiety or fear.</li><li>Anxiety and fear coexist in almost all situations in varying proportions.</li><li>It is more important to find out the causes of your symptoms than to decide if it is fear or anxiety.</li></ul> 

Irrespective of whether anxiety is on the increase or not, it is important that you learn to deal with anxiety in order to lead a more productive and meaningful life. Controlling and preventing anxiety will also enhance your coping skills in case of adversity.

Anxiety is often confused with fear. Box 1 lists the main differences between anxiety and fear.

What are the effects of anxiety?

Anxiety affects everyone, especially when there is excessive mental or emotional stress. It normally leads to two outcomes: (a) intense panic and therefore inability to function normally or adapt to the situations or (b) an ability to anticipate the danger and take appropriate preventive measures against it. The first reaction is called *traumatic anxiety*, and the second reaction is called *signal anxiety*.

What are the causes of anxiety?

All the memories suppressed during the infancy and childhood can have an impact on the adult life and result in anxiety. It is usually the result of an exaggerated response to an emotional stress. Emotional ups and downs are a part of everyone's life. However, some people are more adversely affected by emotional stress than others.

Anxiety often develops over a long period of time and is largely dependent on the entire life's experiences. Specific events or situations can precipitate anxiety attacks but only after a basic pattern of an anxious response to life's experiences is established. There are four main factors that influence development of the pattern of anxious response:

Surroundings
The environment or surroundings in which you live influence the way you think about yourself and others. It could be due to your experiences with family, friends, colleagues, etc. Anxiety is common if you are insecure about your surroundings.

Suppressed emotions
Anxiety can occur if you are unable to find an outlet for your feelings in personal relationships. This is especially true if you suppress anger or frustration for a very long time.

Physical causes
The mind and body are constantly interacting with each other and any change in this interaction may cause anxiety. This is commonly seen in conditions such as pregnancy, adolescence and recovering from

an illness. During these conditions, mood changes are common, and they may lead to anxiety.

Hereditary

Although some emotional disorders may run in families, it is not an important cause of anxiety.

What are the types of anxiety?

Conditions that cause anxiety are broadly divided into three categories: (a) anxiety states, (b) phobic disorders, and (c) post-traumatic stress disorders. The category of anxiety states includes three specific disorders: (i) panic disorders, (ii) generalised anxiety disorder, and (iii) obsessive compulsive disorder.

Anxiety states

Anxiety may either be *acute* (of short duration) or *chronic* (of longer duration). It is common for a person with panic disorder to have symptoms of generalised anxiety disorder. Anxiety without panic attacks is called generalised anxiety disorder. Both panic disorders and generalised disorders have similar causes, signs and symptoms.

What are panic disorders?

Recurrent attacks of anxiety or panic along with nervousness are called panic disorders. They are often associated with a feeling of approaching doom. Panic disorders may either begin slowly with a general feeling of tension and nervous discomfort or occur suddenly with an attack of acute anxiety.

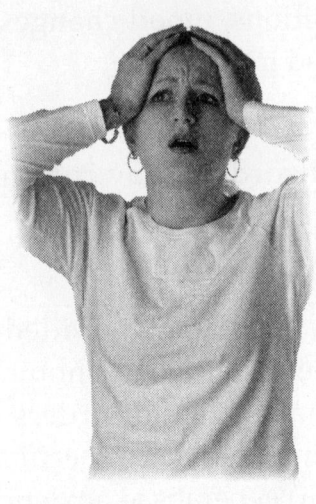
Although panic disorders are more common in young adults, they may also be present in adolescents.

Panic disorders are usually not related to other mental illnesses and often appear to occur without any *precipitating factors*. Precipitating factors are those factors that hasten the onset of signs and symptoms of a disease. You may not be able to recollect or identify precipitating factors of panic attacks, especially if you have suppressed emotions, which a mental health specialist can help you identify.

What are the symptoms of panic disorders?

Common symptoms of panic disorders include a feeling of panic, *palpitations* (thumping sensation and awareness of the heartbeats), pain in the chest, difficulty in, or rapid breathing and a feeling of dizziness or weakness. Most people describe panic as a strange, weird or ghostly feeling — as if something very bad is going to happen.

It is important to remember that you may not always be able to identify the cause of fear and nervousness or the consequences of the event you dread. If you are unable to identify the cause, you are likely to become more desperate and feel that you should do "something" to protect yourself. It may however be difficult to define what this "something" is.

Detailed below are the main symptoms of panic disorders.

Chest pain

Chest pain due to anxiety is often confused with chest pain due to heart attack or angina. There are four major differences between chest pain due to heart problems and anxiety. The chest pain due to anxiety:

1. Lasts only for a few seconds at a time but may repeat every few minutes or hours;
2. Is not related to exercise or physical exertion;
3. Can occur even at rest; and
4. Does not go away when you stop the physical activity which you were doing when the chest pain started.

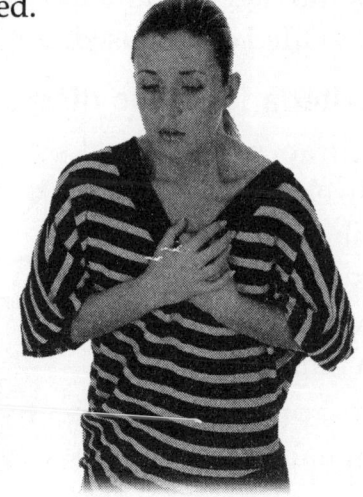

Difficulty in breathing

During an attack of panic, you may begin to breathe more rapidly and more deeply because of the fear that you are inhaling less air. You may also have a strong urge to go out and inhale more air. If the rapid and deep breathing continues for a long time, there may be loss of large amount of carbon dioxide. This imbalance of carbon dioxide in the body is likely to produce additional symptoms such as numbness or tingling in the toes, feet or face, light-headedness and giddiness.

Other symptoms

Some people with anxiety may complain of sensation of heat on the face, sweating, goose pimples and trembling. In addition, there may be pain or hollow butterfly-like fluttering feeling in the stomach. During a panic attack, you may be unable to act or think intelligently and as a result feel as if your mind is clouded or confused.

Diagnostic criteria for panic disorders

- At least three panic attacks within three weeks. These attacks should not be in situations that are related to excessive physical exertion or life-threatening situations.
- Fear and apprehension is present in each panic attack

along with at least four of the following symptoms:
- Difficulty in breathing
- Awareness of, or forceful heartbeats
- Chest pain or discomfort
- Choking or suffocating sensation
- Giddiness or unsteady feeling
- Tingling in the hands and feet
- Feeling of unreality
- Hot and cold flushes
- Sweating
- Faintness
- Trembling or shaking

• Fear of dying, going crazy or mad or doing something uncontrollable during the panic attack.

• At least one attack would have been followed by at least one month of one or more of the following:
- Continuous concern about having another attack(s)
- Significant worry about the likely outcome or consequences of the panic attacks, such as having a heart attack or going crazy
- A major change in behaviour related to the attacks

- No associated physical problems or other mental illnesses such as major depression.

Not associated with fear of being in crowds.

The frequency of panic attacks varies from person to person. Some people may have only a few attacks during the entire life while others may have attacks every few days, weeks or months. Sometimes the panic attacks may stop suddenly without any apparent reason. The severity and duration of symptoms varies with each attack.

What is generalised anxiety disorder?

Generalised anxiety disorder is a condition where there is chronic and exaggerated worry or tension, often without any provocative factors. Most people with this condition live with fear of disaster and worry about most aspects of life such as health, money, family, work, etc. There may be periodic or recurrent acute attacks of panic with more severe symptoms.

Just as in panic disorder, it may not be easy for you to identify the exact cause of generalised anxiety. Even if you do, it is likely that you may not be aware of how and why these troubles cause the symptoms.

What are the signs and symptoms of generalised anxiety disorder?

There are several symptoms of chronic anxiety. Of these, the most common are:

General irritability

Nervousness, irritability, tense and panicky feeling. A chronic worry that an unknown calamity will soon strike leads to sleeplessness and easy tiredness during the day.

Headache

Muscle tension, especially in the head, neck and back, may lead to headache or a dull and throbbing discomfort. The pain may be present either at the back, top or front of the head.

Tremors

Shakiness and trembling of the whole body, especially in the arms and hands.

Increased activity of the autonomic system

Involuntary functions of the body such as breathing, digestion, heartbeats, etc., are called *autonomic functions* as they function independently without outside influence. Anxiety can increase the activity of the autonomic system and therefore lead to increased sweating (especially on the palms of the hand), and flushing of the face. Sometimes there may either be increased dryness or watering in the mouth.

Increased autonomic activity also leads to disturbances in the digestive system. "Butterflies in the stomach" is a very common feeling. Other symptoms include burning sensation in the chest or stomach, fullness in the stomach, which often accompanied by belching, bowel disturbances (especially loose bowels) and increased frequency of passing the urine.

It is important to remember that the progress recovery of generalised anxiety disorder varies from person to person. Some people may recover with short-term treatment, while others may continue to have symptoms and inability to lead a normal life with varying degrees of severity. Chronic anxiety in young adults often tends to become less severe with age, especially if there is success and stability in professional and personal lives.

Diagnostic criteria for generalised anxiety disorder

Generalised anxiety disorder affects no other associated mental disorders such as depression, etc. It strikes people who are eighteen years or above.

Severe and continuous anxiety that has at least three of the following four categories of symptoms are:

Nervous tension

Trembling, shakiness, tension, pain in the muscles, tiredness, inability to relax, twitching of the eyebrows, frowning, strained face, restlessness and restless movements.

General symptoms

Sweating, increased heart rate and palpitations, cold and clammy hands, dry mouth, dizziness, tingling in the hands and feet, increased frequency of passing urine, indigestion, diarrhoea, discomfort in the middle of the stomach, lump in the throat and rapid breathing.

Apprehensive expectations

Anxiety, worry, fear, absentmindedness and anticipation of harm.

Attention

Increased attentiveness that results in distraction, difficulty in concentration, lack of sleep, irritability, impatience and feeling fidgety. No other associated mental disorders such as depression, etc. Continuous anxious mood for at least one month or more.

How are anxiety states diagnosed?

As mentioned earlier, anxiety can also be one of the major symptoms of other psychiatric illnesses. Your doctor will ask several questions to rule out associated disorders.

It is difficult to diagnose anxiety states by physical examination alone. This is because anxiety is normally not associated with abnormalities in any organs or parts of the body. Also, as mentioned earlier, heart rate may be higher and breathing more rapid without any evidence of heart diseases. Thus, the description of your symptoms, especially those related to mental disturbances and/or conflicts, play a critical role in diagnosis of anxiety states. *It is important that you describe all your symptoms, confusions in the mind, doubts, etc., to the doctor very clearly and without any hesitation.* Unless you are frank with your doctor, he/she may not be able to make a correct diagnosis.

Your doctor is likely to recommend a few laboratory tests to rule out conditions such as heart diseases, overactivity of the thyroid gland, disease of the middle ear, etc.

What is the treatment for anxiety states?

Treatment of anxiety states involves four main approaches. These include:
- psychotherapy,
- relaxation therapy,
- meditation, and
- medicines.

Psychotherapy

This term is used for a large number of methods for treating mental and emotional disorders by psychological techniques rather than through medicines or physical treatment. There are two main types of psychotherapy for management of anxiety states. These include *insight psychotherapy* and *supportive psychotherapy*.

Insight psychotherapy involves determination of the strength of the inner self that affects (a) the stability of your relationships with family, friends and working environment, (b) motivation for treatment, and (c) ability to bear difficulties in life. Your doctor will first assess your capacity to "explore" within your mind in order to find out if you are likely to respond to this treatment or not.

If your problem is related to specific and limited situations, you may be free from inner conflicts with short-term therapy and after your doctor has helped to uncover the underlying problems. Freedom from inner conflicts will relieve the symptoms of anxiety.

If the underlying causes are related to neurotic difficulties, psychoanalysis or other similar forms of long-term treatment may be necessary.

Supportive psychotherapy involves discussing your difficulties with your doctor. He/she is likely to reassure you about unrealistic fears and encourage you to face situations and/or circumstances that lead to anxiety. Although supportive psychotherapy will not cure anxiety, it will help you understand the situations that lead to anxiety and change them in order to reduce stress.

Relaxation therapy

Relaxation techniques can be helpful if you are eager to accept suggestions from your doctor and implement them. He/she may teach you specific relaxation techniques. It is important that you practise these techniques under your doctor's guidance initially so that both of you are confident that you are able to practise correct relaxation techniques. *It is important to remember that a daily routine of these relaxation techniques is necessary for controlling anxiety.* You should also practise them whenever you feel the inner tension rising or when faced with situations that normally lead to anxiety.

Meditation

Transcendental meditation or other simple forms of meditation that are not related to religious rituals or practices are likely to relieve symptoms of anxiety. Several research studies worldwide have indicated that meditation helps maintain an optimum level of the involuntary functions of the body (such as heart rate, respiration, digestion, etc.).

Medicines

Your doctor may prescribe mild *tranquillisers* and *antidepressants* to reduce the symptoms of anxiety. Tranquillisers are medicines that calm agitated or anxious people without affecting the consciousness. Antidepressants are medicines that relieve depression by restoring the balance of chemical substances in the nervous system. Detailed below are some of the common medicines used for management of anxiety states.

Benzodiazepines

There are several medicines in this group of tranquillisers. *Diazepam* is one of the common medicines in this group. It is a long-acting medicine, is rapidly absorbed in the stomach and begins to act within fifteen to twenty minutes. However, the maximum effect is observed only one to two hours after taking the medicine. Absorption of diazepam injection is very slow and erratic. It is therefore usually not given. *Lorazepam*, another medicine in this group, is absorbed slowly and gives maximum effect after two hours. Unlike diazepam injection, lorazepam injection is absorbed rapidly.

Common side effects of benzodiazepines include tiredness and drowsiness, especially in the initial stages. *It is therefore important that you avoid driving vehicles or working near a dangerous machine after taking these medicines.*

Benzodiazepines are addictive, especially if taken continuously for more than three months. They are also not recommended during pregnancy and breast-feeding as it may adversely affect the unborn baby and the infant respectively. Box 2 details the symptoms and principles of withdrawal of benzodiazepines.

Alprazolam

In recent times, this medicine has been used very extensively for management of anxiety and some other mental illnesses. Although its impact on anxiety is similar to those of benzodiazepines, alprazolam results in less severe side effects, especially drowsiness. This is also an addictive medicine.

Box 2. Withdrawal of Benzodiazepines

Symptoms

- Anxiety
- Irritability or depression
- Nausea
- Numbness or tingling sensation in the limbs
- Pain and weakness in muscles
- Difficulty in sleeping
- Confusion
- Fits or seizures

Principles of withdrawal

- Dose of medicine to be reduced gradually.
- The dose to be reduced by 10-25% of daily dose once in two weeks.
- Dose to be reduced only if symptoms are absent.
- If symptoms recur with reduced dose, relaxation techniques to be practiced and/or alternative medicines to be used.
- Short-acting medicine to be replaced temporarily with long-acting medicine.

Buspirone

This is one of the newer medicines for management of anxiety. Although its effect on anxiety is similar to that of diazepam, buspirone does not result in addiction or withdrawal symptoms. Its action is slower and the maximum effect is normally observed after three to four weeks. Buspirone is therefore recommended for chronic anxiety.

Several research studies are resulting in rapid changes in the understanding and applications of the medicines used for treatment of anxiety. It is therefore advisable that you avoid self-medication and take medicines as per your doctor's prescription only.

It is important to remember that although medicines can relieve symptoms temporarily, they cannot cure anxiety. You should therefore consult with a mental health specialist to resolve the conflicts and problems that cause anxiety. Irrespective of how long it takes you to overcome the root cause of the anxiety, you should continue efforts to develop an ability to deal with stress and conflicts more effectively.

Phobic disorders

Phobic disorders are conditions where you have irrational fears of a specific object, activity or situation. This fear results in a strong urge to avoid them. The irrational fears are called *phobias* and conditions with phobias are called phobic disorders.

Phobias have three main features:
1. The fear is disproportionate to the circumstances.
2. You cannot deal with the fear by reasoning or control it with will power.
3. You are aware that your fears are not justified and yet you stay away from the feared object, activity or situation.

Many people have simple phobias such as fear of animals, high places or closed rooms. You can easily manage these fears by avoiding them. However, some phobias are extreme and serious. They result in anxiety and often lead to panic. Several million people worldwide are estimated to have severe phobias and panic attacks as a result of them.

What are the types of phobias?

There are three main types of phobic disorders. These include *simple phobia* (fear of objects), *social phobia* (fear of functions) and *agoraphobia* (fear of situations).

Phobias usually do not adversely affect the life in adulthood. This is because the fear is often specific and avoiding the cause of fear may not be critical for professional and personal development. The term "phobic disorder" is used when the phobias result in significant symptoms and disability of varying degrees.

Agoraphobia and simple phobia are more common among women. Agoraphobia and social phobia may be present in several members of a family.

What are the symptoms of simple phobia?

An irrational fear of objects is called simple phobia. It normally occurs during infancy and early childhood, which are the early stages of growth and development. Simple phobia may persist till adult life and may appear again after a period of no symptoms. Simple phobia has three essential and one associated features. Essential features include:

- Fear of a specific object or situation that is not related to situations or functions;
- Tendency to avoid situations that you feel can lead to anxiety; and
- Sudden exposure to the object you fear may produce a panic attack.

A likely associated feature is the tendency to seek detailed information on a situation that you fear before you actually face the situation.

Diagnostic criteria for simple phobia

- Continuous irrational fear of, or a forceful desire to avoid an object or situation such as animals, heights, closed rooms, receiving injections, seeing blood, etc.

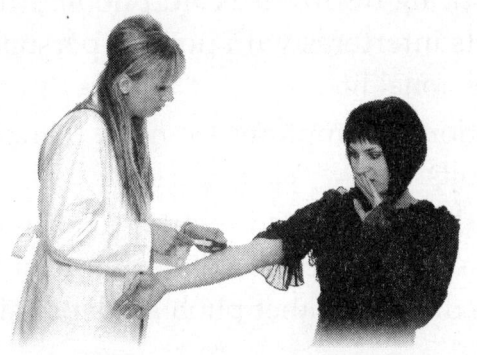

- Exposure to the phobic situation or object often results in panic attacks. Children may express anxiety due to simple phobia by crying, throwing tantrums, clinging, etc. Recognition, especially by adults, that the fear is either excessive or unreasonable, often causes excessive distress.

- The strong desire to avoid phobic situations or objects interferes with normal personal and/or professional life.
- Duration of symptoms for more than six months in adults.
- No other associated mental disorders such as obsessive compulsive disorder, post-traumatic stress disorder, other phobias, depression, etc.

What is agoraphobia?

Fear of being in a situation where you may either be helpless or humiliated, especially during an attack of panic, is called agoraphobia. People with agoraphobia are scared of being away from help or a secure place such as home. They have two types of fears: fear of some specific situations and fear of fear itself. This means that you will anticipate a panic attack. This anticipation or fear of panic attacks leads to more and more such situations. As the frequency of these fears increase, you are likely to behave in a way that proves that your fears were correct. At this stage, you may become scared to go out of the house alone, travel or be in a situation from where you cannot get away quickly. Thus, agoraphobia is a vicious cycle that increases the intensity of the fear itself.

Agoraphobia is estimated to be ten times more common among women than men. This is perhaps because the way most women are brought up, they tend to become insecure and dependent. A large proportion of women are overprotected during their childhood, are "taught" not to assert themselves. They are also not often provided with opportunities to exhibit their skills, special talents, etc., or develop confidence.

What are the symptoms of agoraphobia?

Agoraphobia has three essential and two associated features. Essential features include:

1. Irrational fear of leaving familiar surroundings of the home;
2. Symptoms of anxiety usually appear after an acute attack of panic, which leads to anticipation of helplessness away from home; and
3. Fear of being in crowded and closed spaces and tunnels, or any other situation where access to help is limited.

Associated features include:
- Pleading, demanding, manipulative or child-like behaviour, and
- A tendency for obsessive behaviour.

Diagnostic criteria for agoraphobia
- Significant fear of being alone in public places from where escape or help may not be easily

available. These include crowds, tunnels, bridges and public transportation.

- A strong desire to avoid situations described above.
- Gradual restriction to normal activities till the desire to avoid situations described above begins to adversely affect the life.
- Symptoms are not due to normal side effects of medicines or any other abnormal health condition.
- No other associated mental illnesses.

What are the signs and symptoms of social phobia?
Fear of behaving in a manner that can invite ridicule from others is called social phobia. It occurs less frequently than simple phobia or agoraphobia.

Social phobia has three essential and three associated features. Essential features include:
1. Fear of situations in which you may be exposed to scrutiny or critical observations by others.
2. Excessive anxiety of being criticised or ridiculed when forced to be in situations where others can "inspect" you.
3. Anxiety is mainly due to fear of behaving in a shameful manner in front of others.

Associated features include:
1. Awareness that others may recognise signs of anxiety when you are forced to be in situations where they can "inspect" you.
2. Anxiety may adversely affect your behaviour and/or performance, thus increasing the intensity of anxiety.
3. Occasionally you may have generalised anxiety without any apparent cause.

Diagnostic criteria for social phobia

- A persistent, irrational fear of being exposed to situations where
  - others may scrutinise you, and
  - you may behave in a shameful manner.
- A strong desire to avoid situations described above.
- Stressed feeling because you recognise that your fear is either unreasonable or excessive.
- No other associated mental illness.

What is the treatment for phobic disorders?

There are four main approaches to management of phobic disorders. These include: (a) psychotherapy, (b) behaviour therapy, (c) medicines, and (d) supportive therapy.

Psychotherapy

In this approach, your doctor will help you identify the root cause of your phobias and analyse them for you. It is important to remember that the psychological techniques for management of phobic disorders are effective only if you are receptive to these methods of treatment. If you are not, even after identifying and analysing your inner conflicts, you may continue to have symptoms of phobias.

Behaviour therapy

In recent times, this approach, which involves techniques that influence and change your behaviour, has been demonstrated to be very effective. One of these techniques involves desensitising you from the phobias. Your doctor will expose you, one after another, to the images of a predetermined list of situations, objects or conditions that cause phobias. He/she will first begin with a cause that is likely to cause least symptoms and combine this image with one that is associated with pleasant sensations. If these pleasant sensations are strong, they can suppress the anxiety. Your doctor may also prescribe tranquillisers for a short duration and teach you simple methods of muscle relaxation that you can practice whenever you are exposed to phobic situations. Once you are "desensitised" to this phobia, the doctor will repeat the exercise with successive phobic images, moving gradually from those that cause least symptoms to those that cause severe symptoms. Another successful behavioural technique is intensive exposure to either the cause of phobia or its image as long as you are able to tolerate the fear until a time when there is no more fear.

Behavioural therapy is more effective for social and simple phobia rather than for agoraphobia. It is however important to remember that the results of this approach vary from person to person.

Medicines

Your doctor may prescribe an antidepressant, especially if you have agoraphobia. Just as for anxiety states, several medicines are recommended *temporarily* for management of phobias in order to relieve symptoms. Once anxiety subsides, it is easier to resolve inner conflicts.

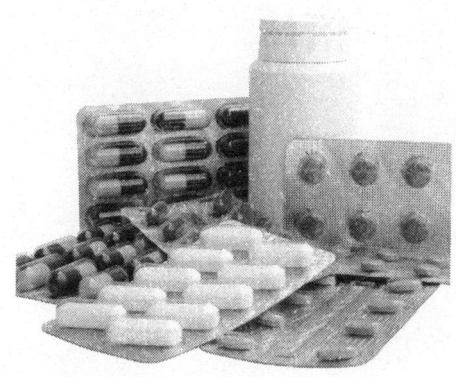

Supportive therapy

Supportive behaviour from the doctor, family and friends can reduce the symptoms and make other approaches of treatment more effective. It is important to remember that the more you avoid what you fear, more intense is your fear likely to be. Supportive therapy can help you develop confidence to deal with the fears over a period of time.

Irrespective of the cause of anxiety, you can control the symptoms by adopting a positive attitude towards life and developing a regular routine of exercises and relaxation techniques such as meditation.

Ayurveda

It is amazing that the man lives a life of worry, anxiety and discontentment in the midst of prosperity. This is a contradiction and therefore Ayurveda aims at happy state of life. It lays emphasis on the need to overcome this duality by appreciating the methods and measures to regulate and control obstacles such as desire, anger, pride, greed, etc.

Ayurveda has recognised the individuality of the psyche and body and their inseparable and dependent relationship in the living body.

Categories of abnormal mental functions as per Ayurveda

The classification of Manovikaras as per the classical literature are :

Impairment of general mental functions are given below:
- Abnormalities in the perceptions and control of involuntary of the body in the absence of any abnormality of the organs (*Indriya Vigrah*)
- Mental control (*Manonigraha*)
- Guess (*Ooha*)
- Thought and different aspects of the mind (*Vichara*)
- Decision (*Buddhi*)
- Memory (*Smriti*)
- Orientation and responsiveness (*Sanjajnana*)
- Desire (*Bhakti*)
- Habit and Temperament (*Shula*)
- Psychomotor activity (*Chesta*)
- Conduct, separately or in combination (*Achara*)
- Weak mind (the presence of *Alpasatva*) in the origin of the illness
- Involvement of the three doshas of the body on the two doshas of the mind or two doshas of the mind alone.
- Classical identification of the disease either as

mental disorder (*Manosvikaran*) or disorders of the mind and body (*Ubhayatmakvikara*)
- Contamination of *manovaha stotas*

What are the symptoms of anxiety?

The term *Chittodvega* has special reference to Manovikaras and can be equated with anxiety. It is commonly observed in people who have instability of the mind, fear, tremor, palpitation, short temper, indecisiveness, pressure in the chest, fainting or sinking, pricking pain in the chest and excessive perspiration. According to Charaka, the famous physician of ancient times, these symptoms are due to contamination of *vata*. There is imbalance of two mental doshas (*rajas* and *tamas*) and abnormalities *vata* and/or *pitta*.

Clinical signs and symptoms of anxiety as per Ayurvedic literature

- Fear
- Diffidence of lack of resolution
- Tremor or fine shivering of the hands
- Palpitations or awareness of the heartbeats
- Irritability or short temper
- Excessive sweat
- Increased thirst

- Dryness of the mouth
- Dryness of the throat
- Constricting feeling in the chest
- Ficklemindedness or restlessness
- Fatigue
- Expansion by pulling of the muscles of the face and neck
- Poor memory
- Negative thinking
- Body ache

What is the treatment for anxiety?

Ayurveda recommends a combination of medicines for internal administration and external applications. These medicines are in addition to counselling or treatment of the psyche and behaviour. The treatment processes commonly recommended for management of anxiety include purgatives, enema, nasal instillation, streaming of medicated buttermilk, milk, oil or decoctions on the forehead and application of medicated wet cakes on the head.

Listed below are the compound medicines commonly used for management of anxiety.

1. Five grams of any one of the three medicines including *Brahmi Ghrita, Kalyanak Ghrita* or *Pahchagavya Ghrita* to be taken twice a day with milk.
2. Twenty to thirty millilitres of either *Saraswatarista* or *Aswagandharista* to be taken after meals twice a day with equal proportion of water.
3. One hundred and twenty-five to two hundred and fifty milligrams of either *Smriti Sagar Rasa* or *Cahurmukha Rasa* to be taken with honey two or three times a day.
4. Three to five grams of *Saraswata Churna* thrice a day with milk.
5. One hundred and twenty-five to two hundred and fifty milligrams of *Manasmitra Vataka* to be taken with water or milk thrice a day.

6. Five millilitres of *Ksheerbala Tail* to be taken orally with milk three times a day.
7. *Dhanvantari Tail* or *Asanvilvadi Tail* is recommended for causing profuse sweating, and therefore removal of toxins from the body.
8. Tonics recommended for anxiety include any one of the following medicines: *Kusumanda rasayana, Chayavanprash, Brahmi rasayana, Asvagandhavaleha* or *Shatavari Leha*. Depending on the totality of your symptoms, ten grams of any one of these medicines is recommended once a day with milk.

Homoeopathy

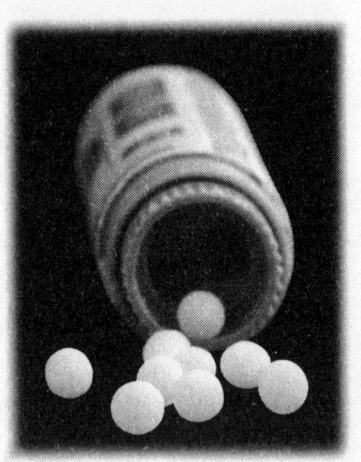

Homoeopathy defines anxiety as the result of an insecure mind reacting to circumstances that are apparently adverse to a person but are not openly threatening. The sense of fear is more internal than external. However, it is sufficiently strong to lead to attacks of apprehension.

Everyone reacts with anxiety at some time or the other and this is quite in harmony with normal life. Some people, however, begin to have anxiety as a routine than as an exception and therefore adversely affect their life. It is then necessary to consult a doctor who can help overcome the anxiety.

What is the Homoeopathic approach to anxiety?

Homoeopathy offers a wide range of medicines that are effective in the management of anxiety. These medicines are neither sedative nor do they suppress the symptoms. They bring "out" the symptoms and remove them completely. Just as in Allopathy, a Homoeopath will also try to find out the root cause behind anxiety attacks and prescribe appropriate medicines that can overcome apprehensions. You will therefore gain emotional strength.

Just as in all diseases, a detailed case history plays a very important role in selecting medicines that are most suited to you and in a strength and dose that is most effective. It is therefore important that you talk to the doctor very frankly and share all your troubles and problems. The doctor will of course keep your conversations with him/her confidential. Detailed below are the questions that your doctor is likely to ask you.

Precipitating factors

You should describe the immediate circumstances that occur just before an anxiety attack. These could be emotional shock such as loss of a close friend or family member, poor examination results, setbacks in business or other professions, financial loss, etc. These situations make you vulnerable and you may not be able to cope with even minor ups and downs of life.

Past history

Any emotional setback in the past (such as those described above) can also weaken your resistance to deal with adverse circumstances. This weakness may result in your over-reacting to even minor situations in life. You should also describe if there were specific cases of fright, grief or suppressed emotions in your childhood. This is because these childhood experiences can weaken your personality and you may therefore not be able to deal with the pressures of life and succumb to anxiety.

Physical ailments

Any long-term illness can weaken your natural defence mechanism. You are therefore likely to be physically and emotionally weak.

Family background

Children of parents who are prone to anxiety attacks are more likely to adopt the same type of behaviour. These children therefore develop anxious personality as they grow up. Similarly, when one of the parents is too dominating or aggressive, the child becomes timid. Such children are more likely to be adversely affected by the pressures of living.

Lack of parental love, loss of a loved one at a young age, neglect due to various circumstances and constraints, etc., lead to lack of confidence in a person. Such people are also prone to become apprehensive and anxious.

Circumstances at school, college or place of work

An emotionally insecure or timid person normally finds it difficult to deal with challenging situations such as examinations, interviews, submission of project reports, etc., either at school, college or place of work. Such people find it very difficult to cope with these situations and develop anxiety or panic attacks. Sometimes teachers and/or colleagues may harass the weak people, thus reducing whatever little confidence they have.

Basic nature

Your basic nature is very important. Some people are basically weak and react with anxiety even to minor situations whereas some others are emotionally strong and remain cool even in the most difficult circumstances. All of us are equipped with "fight or flight" reaction and react according to whichever feature is more dominant.

Presenting symptoms

Your symptoms at the time of visiting the doctor are also very important. You should make notes of any changes in your normal behaviour, unnatural fears, phobias, panic reactions, etc., and describe them to the doctor. You should also describe changes in your general habits such as likes and dislikes, food habits, sensitivity to weather, etc. Finally, you should describe physical symptoms such as diarrhoea, constipation, acidity, skin problems, hair fall, etc.

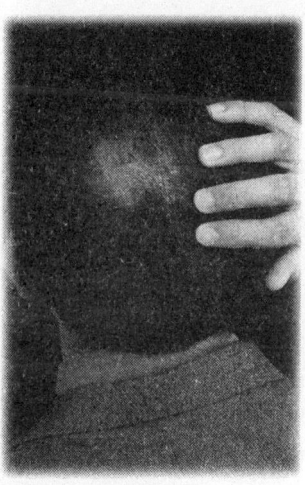

Your doctor will collectively evaluate all your symptoms before prescribing appropriate medicines in the dose and strength that are likely to relieve symptoms rapidly and without any side effects.

What is the treatment for anxiety?

Detailed below are some of the medicines that are more commonly used to manage anxiety.

Arsenic album

This is one of the most important medicines used in the management of anxiety. Symptoms that respond well to this medicine are anxiety over small, trivial situations, associate fear or death or disease, intense mental restlessness and general physical weakness. In addition, there may be dryness of the mouth and you may need to sip water very frequently.

Aconite

This medicine is effective for severe fear and anxiety resulting from past experience of fright or shock.

Argentum nitricum and Gelsimium

Both these medicines are useful in cases of anxiety in anticipation of meetings, interviews, exams, etc. Some people develop loose motions in anticipation of such situations.

Kali phos

This medicine is commonly used for treating insomnia due to anxiety. It is usually prescribed in a biochemic form, which is, as tablets in low potencies.

Natrum mur and Ignatia
Both these medicines are very effective in managing anxiety when there is history of grief. It is especially effective for people who are usually reserved and do not express their sorrow. They are more likely to brood over situations and become anxious.

Aurum met
This medicine is very effective for people who have anxiety with depression, to the extent that they become suicidal.

Staphysagria
It is effective if anxiety and depression is the result of suppressed emotions or indignation over unmerited insults.

Tranquil
This is a biochemic compound that is effective in treating anxiety without any apparent cause.

The present day life-style predisposes to immense stress and there is hardly a person who can claim to be free of anxiety in some form or the other. Homoeopathic medicines such as Tranquil are very effective in controlling the adverse effects of these stresses.

What are the advantages of Homoeopathy?
Homoeopathic medicines used for management of anxiety have three main advantages:

No side effects

Homoeopathic medicines are not sedatives and therefore do not cause side effects such as drowsiness, dullness of mind, etc. They act by enhancing your potential to fight anxiety and become emotionally stronger.

Treatment of physical ailments

Homoeopathic medicines also cure physical effects of anxiety such as hair fall, acidity, skin diseases, headaches, etc. This is of course in addition to their main action of removing the root cause of anxiety — emotional disturbances.

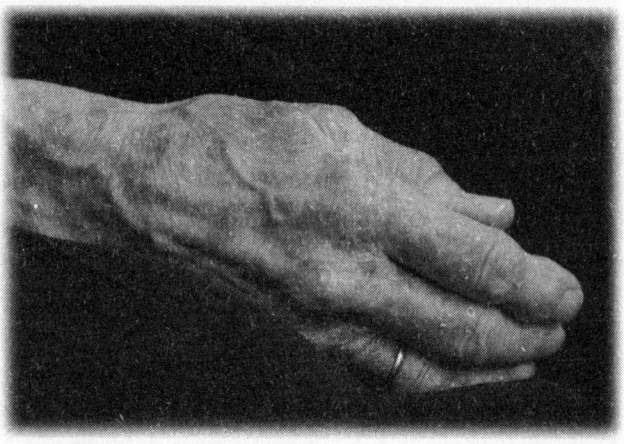

Sense of well-being

Homoeopathic medicines give an almost immediate sense of well-being and are not addictive. With these medicines you can improve the quality of your life, feel active and fresh and at the same time not become dependent on medicines.

In addition to prescribing medicines, your Homoeopath will also act as a counsellor. He/she will counsel you and your family by making you aware of the reasons behind the behavioural changes and help you to come to term with your natural potential.

Nature Cure

Causes of anxiety, its types and signs and symptoms of each of these types as per Nature Cure are the same as those detailed in the section on Allopathy.

According to Nature Cure, the blood vessels and nerves of an anxious person become numb and hard. As a result, there is obstruction in the free flow of blood and nerve currents. Thus, the inflow of the vital forces of the body is either reduced or shut down. Reduced flow of vital forces lowers the natural resistance to poisons in the body and other disease causing agents. In extreme conditions when anxiety and associated fear is very intense, the obstruction to the flow of vital forces can lead to death.

What is the treatment for anxiety?

Nature Cure recommends relaxation techniques, supportive behaviour and reassurance from friends and family, exercises and diet for management of anxiety. In case of severe or long-standing anxiety, counselling and other forms of treatment from a mental health specialist may be necessary. It is also important to live in a congenial atmosphere with fresh air, sunshine, calm and quiet place for relaxation and exercises and eat natural food. Above all, there is a need to develop self-control that will enable you to remain calm in moments of stress and tension.

Self-control

The only sure method to control anxiety is to relax. Try to analyse the conditions or situations that cause anxiety and identify options or solutions. Adopt any one option or solution that **you** believe is most suited to you. Try to develop a positive attitude.

Support

Support from family and friends may provide temporary relief but it cannot prevent or cure anxiety. Seek their help to identify solutions and implement them. Their support will also help you to take up activities that interest you and help you direct your mind in gainful ways.

Physical measures

Treatment options with air, water, mud and exercises, especially yoga, are very effective for development of positive attitude and for relaxation.

- **Exercises:** Exercise improves blood circulation, especially to the skin, clears the blood channels and maintains normal conditions of the nerves. It also reduces congestion to the brain and other organs of the body.
- **Deep breathing:** It is one of the most effective methods of relaxation. You can do it either while sitting or lying down, with both the nostrils or alternate nostrils. You should learn the correct method of deep breathing from a qualified person. If the technique is not correct, you may not have any benefits. You can practice deep breathing in the morning on empty stomach, just before going to sleep and whenever you feel exhausted, stressed or anxious during the day.
- **Water and mud treatments:** They are also very effective for relaxation and soothing irritated nerves.

Sleep

Sleeping for six to eight hours in the night will restore the energy you have spent during the day. Regular practice of meditation, *shavasana* (a type of yoga) and deep breathing will help you sleep better.

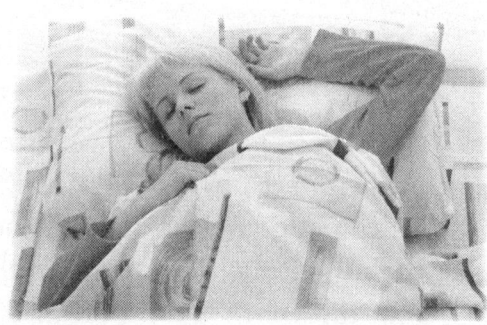

It is important to remember that you should sleep about two to three hours after dinner so that the food is digested.

Music

Several research studies have persuasively indicated that listening to soft music can relax the mind and hasten recovery during illness.

Diet

Just as for all health problems, Nature Cure lays special emphasis on diet. It is desirable to avoid adulterated and processed foods as they increase the production of "poisons" in the body. These poisons contaminate the blood and therefore irritate and reduce efficiency of various organs of the body. Natural foods are preferable.

Anxiety often leads to indigestion. This is because of
- improper chewing of the food, and
- reduced production of the digestive juices by irritated organs of the digestive system. Irrespective of the food intake, you will feel sick most of the times because of indigestion.

Avoid excess intake of starch, protein and fat such as oil, *ghee*, butter, etc., as they adversely affect normal chemical processes in the body. Eat foods that are rich in potassium, calcium, magnesium and iron. You should also avoid irritants such as condiments and spices, chillies, pickles, etc.

Your Nature Cure doctor may recommend fasting or a juice diet for a few days in order to remove "poisons" from the body.

Treatments for anxiety

The following treatment options are effective for relaxation and soothing irritated nerves.

Neutral bath

Lie down in a bathtub filled with water slightly cooler than the body temperature (about 92-95° F) for thirty minutes to an hour. Neutral bath reduces the irritation of the nerves of the skin and therefore, results in a calm and relaxed feeling.

Full wet-sheet pack

Wrap the body with a wet cloth dipped in cold water and cover it with a blanket. Keeping the full wet-sheet pack for thirty to forty-five minutes relaxes the body and mind.

Cold water

Allow a stream of cold water to fall on the entire body for two to three minutes. Cold water shower results in relaxation by soothing the nerve endings of the skin.

Hot and cold application

Pouring hot water or doing hot fomentation of the backbone for five to ten minutes followed by pouring cold water or doing cold fomentation of the backbone for fifteen to twenty seconds results in relaxation.

Cold spinal bath

Lie down in a tub partially filled with cold water in such a way that only the backbone comes in contact with the water. In addition to relaxation, cold spinal bath for thirty to forty-five minutes every day also strengthens the nervous system.

Foot bath

Alternate hot and cold foot bath is also an effective method for relaxation. Pour hot water on the feet for three minutes followed by cold water for thirty seconds. Instead of pouring water, you can also immerse the feet in hot and cold water alternately for the same duration.

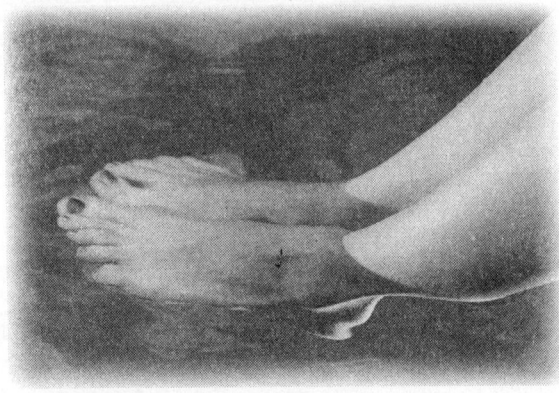

Warm bath

A warm bath just before you go to bed will help you relax and sleep well.

Cold pack

A cold pack to the back of hand and neck provides good relaxation.

Walking

Walking bare foot on the snow or dew reduces congestion of the brain and therefore results in relaxation.

Massage

A whole body massage relaxes the tense muscles and nerves of the body.

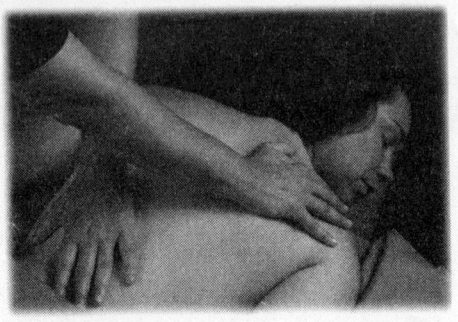

Mud bath

Application of mud on the body once or twice a week relaxes the mind.

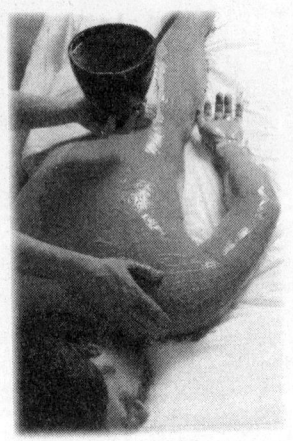

Blue light

Using blue light in the bedroom also relaxes the mind.

Unani

Anxiety is known as "Izterab" in the Unani system of medicine. It is defined as a "melancholic" disorder that is caused by excessive secretion of *sauda* (melancholic humour). This excessive secretion adversely affects the faculty that controls the nervous system, called *Quwat Nafsania*. There are three main factors that adversely affect the five latent faculties of the brain, called *Quwa khams Batina*.

These include:

- excessive secretion of black bile or melancholic humour,
- transformation of abnormally digested *safravi* (Choleric) or *Balghami* (Phlegmatic) humours into abnormal melancholic humour, and
- transformation in the normal quality of the melancholic humour.

What are the signs and symptoms of anxiety?

In the early stage of the disorder, you may feel discomfort with fear and mild depression. If the condition lasts for a long time, symptoms such as pain in the muscles, headache, shivering of the hands, palpitation, diarrhoea, sweating, breathlessness or difficulty in breathing, dizziness, unstable walk, a sensation of swinging or hanging in the space, walking on the sky, flying in the air, etc., may be present.

What are the principles of treatment of anxiety?

There are four main Unani principles for treatment of anxiety. These include:

1. Correction of factors that result in excessive production of melancholic humour or change its normal quality through diet, exercises, mental work, habits, etc.
2. Reduction of the load or stress on the faculty controlling the nervous system by sedating it with *Mukhadirat* (sedatives).
3. Taking coctives and purgatives for black bile or melancholic humour.
4. Strengthening the faculty that controls the nervous system by giving *Muqawwi at Asab Wa Dimagh* or tonics of the nervous system.

What is the treatment for anxiety?

Detailed below are the commonly used single and compound medicines for treatment of anxiety including their method of use:
- Oil of lettuce seeds or bottle-gourd seeds to be applied on the head.
- One or two tablets of *Dawul Shifa* to be taken twice or thrice a day with *Arq-e-shivneez*.
- One to two tablets of *Hab Jawahar Mohra* to be twice or thrice a day.
- Make a fine powder of three grams each of Stoechados (*Ustukhudus*) and coriander along with five grains of black pepper. This medicine is recommended with water early in the morning on empty stomach. You need to rest in the bed for half an hour to one hour after taking this medicine.
- Make a fine powder of ten grams each of flowers of Babool, coriander and seeds of bottle gourd. This preparation is recommended three grams of the powder with water twice a day.
- Boil six grams each of *jatamansi,* cinnamon and dry ginger in one hundred and twenty millilitres of water. Strain the liquid and add saccharine. This preparation is recommended in the morning on empty stomach.
- Make a fine powder separately of five hundred milligrams of camphor and two grams of ammonium chloride. Mix the two powders well

and store in a clean and airtight glass bottle and use it as an inhaler.
- Make a fine powder of equal proportions of opium, myrrh and cinnamon. Add some water to make a paste. This paste is applied on the cloth and placed on one or both sides of the head just above the cheekbones.

- Seven grams of either *Itrifal Ustukhudus* or *Itrifal Kkishneezi* is recommended at bedtime.
- Ten grams of *Itrifal Zamani* is recommended at bedtime.
- Six grams of *Khamira Gaozaban Amberi* is recommended in the morning before breakfast.
- *Qurs Musallae* is rubbed in water and the paste applied on the forehead.
- Three grams of *Barshasha* is recommended whenever you have any pain associated with anxiety.

Ten helpful tips to cope with anxiety

1. Forget about past problems and situations and concentrate on the present.
2. Learn to differentiate between real and irrational fears, and chase out the irrational fears from your mind.
3. Be confident and confront your fears.
4. Think positively and act courageously. Have faith in yourself.
5. Concentrate on your interests first. Remember that no one else will protect your interests as well as you.

6. Develop new habits in dealing with stress. You can do this with discipline and practice.
7. Learn how to say 'no'. It takes courage to stand up for your convictions and principles.
8. Take a balanced diet and do regular exercises to maintain health because physical and emotional health are interlinked.
9. Learn how to make decisions that suit you most and stick to them.
10. In case your doctor recommends medicines, take them to get temporary relief. Try to discuss the causes of your anxiety with the doctor.

Definitions

Antidepressants are medicines that relieve depression by restoring the balance of chemical in the nervous system.

Autonomic functions are those that function independently without outside influence.

Panic is a sudden overpowering fright accompanied by a strong desire or attempts to secure safety.

Physiological means related to the process of normal functions of the body.

Precipitating factors are those that hasten the onset of signs and symptoms of a disease.

Psychological means related to the behaviour, functions and processes of the mind.

Tranquillisers are medicines that calm agitated or anxious people without affecting the consciousness.

References

Allopathy

Kaplan, Harold, Benjamin, Dadock, Ed. *Comprehensive Textbook of Psychiatry*, Williams and Wilkins, Baltimore, London, 1994.

Ayurveda

Chaturvedi, G. N. *Charaka Samhita — Hindi Commentary*.

Shastry, Ravi, Amritadatta Roy, *Sushrut Samhita — Hindi Commentary*.

Ramu, M. G., B. S. Venkataraman and Janakiramaiah, Manovikar with special references to Udvega (Anxiety) and Vishada (Depression), *NIMHANS Journal* 6(1), January 1998, pp 41-46.

Ramu, M.G. and B.S. Venkataraman, Manovikar (mental disorders) in Ayurveda, *Ancient Science of Life*, Vol. IV, No. 3 January 1984, pp 165-173.

Nature Cure

Diamond, Harvey and Marilyn, *Fit for Life* — Part II

Graham, Arthur Dr., *Depression and Anxiety*

Henry, Dr., *Practice of Natural Therapeutics*

Kalloy, JH., *Rational Hydrotherapy*

Sokolov, E I, V P Podactin and E V Belova. *Emotional Stress and Cardiovascular Response*

Vogel, A. Swiss *Nature Doctor*

Health Solutions

ANXIETY

DIABETES

FIRST AID

HEART ATTACK

HIV/AIDS

MENOPAUSE

MENSTRUAL IRREGULARITIES

NUTRITION